A Closer Walk with God

Developing A Christian Lifestyle

Leader's Guide

Billie Hanks, Jr.
and
William A. Shell

WORD MINISTRY RESOURCES

"Grow in the grace and knowledge of our Lord and Savior Jesus Christ."
(NCV) 2 Peter 3:18

The CHRISTIAN ESSENTIALS Series

A Bible Study Leader's Guide

Available from:
Word Ministry Resources
P.O. Box 2518   Waco, TX   76702-2518   (800) 933-9673

Copyright © 1992 by International Evangelism Association
P.O. Box 6499   Fort Worth, TX   76115-6499   (817) 926-8465
All Rights Reserved

No part of this publication may be reproduced or transmitted in any form, electronic or mechanical, including photocopy, recording, or any informational storage system, without permission in writing from the publisher.

Those passages marked NCV are from *The Holy Bible, New Century Version*, copyright © 1987, 1988, 1991 by Word Publishing, Dallas, Texas 75039.

Scripture quotations identified NASB are from *The New American Standard Bible*, copyright © 1960, 1962, 1971, 1972, 1973, 1975, by the Lockman Foundation and used by permission.

Scripture passages identified as KJV are from *The Holy Bible*, King James Version, copyright © 1972 by Thomas Nelson, Inc., Publishers.

Those passages marked NKJV are from *The New King James Bible*, copyright © 1979 by Thomas Nelson, Inc., Publishers.

Scripture quotations identified NIV are from *The Holy Bible: New International Version*, copyright © 1978 by the New York International Bible Society. Used by permission of Zondervan Bible Publishers.

CONTENTS

Introduction To the *Leader's Guide* 1

SESSION	1	– Hearing God's Word 8
SESSION	2	– Reading God's Word 12
SESSION	3	– Studying and Memorizing God's Word . 15
SESSION	4	– Meditation and Application 17
SESSION	5	– The Priviledge of Prayer 20
SESSION	6	– Five Ways to Pray 23
SESSION	7	– The Making of a Disciple 25
SESSION	8	– The First Century Vision 28
SESSION	9	– Steps Toward a Discipling Ministry 31
SESSION	10	– Sharing the Truth in Love 34
SESSION	11	– Sharing My Personal Story 36
SESSION	12	– Sharing God's Plan of Salvation 39
SESSION	13	– Living By Faith 43

APPENDICES

A. **The Public and Private Ministry of Jesus** 45
B. **Spiritual Friendship with New Christians** 47
C. **The Burden of My Heart** 51
D. **Sharing Christ Naturally** 62
E. **My Personal Conversion Story** 63
F. **The Indwelling Christ** 65
G. **Lesson Illustrations** 68

"You shall love the Lord your God with all your heart,
with all your soul, and with all your might"
DEUTERONOMY 6:5 (NKJV).

ACKNOWLEDGMENTS

"As iron sharpens iron, so one man sharpens another"
(PROVERBS 27:17)

We thank each dedicated friend and colleague who has helped make this course possible — by praying, believing, working, and field testing ***The Christian Essentials Series***!

INTRODUCTION

"As you therefore have received Christ Jesus as Lord, so walk in Him"
(COLOSSIANS 2:6, NASB).

MINISTRY PURPOSE

May God richly bless you and your group as you learn to walk more closely with Him!

The spiritual purpose for teaching *A Closer Walk with God* is to acquaint those in your group with the basics of living the Christian life more effectively and consistently. The biblical content of this course is designed to provide a *motivational* and *equipping* experience for any member of any church.

Five major aspects of the Christian life will be studied and applied during the course. These *life-changing* subjects include:

- **Internalizing God's Word**
- **The Privilege of Prayer**
- **The Making of a Disciple**
- **Sharing the Truth in Love**
- **Living By Faith**

In addition, three inspiring *spiritual disciplines* will be taught and practiced during the course. These include:

- **Learning to take effective sermon and Bible study notes**
- **Developing a rich and rewarding daily *Quiet Time***
- **Beginning a life long commitment to scripture memory**

By the conclusion of this course, class members will have received the inspiration and training needed to build and sustain a closer personal walk with God. They will have also learned the fundamentals of *witnessing naturally*.

Experience has shown that a high percentage of your class graduates will be ready to receive more advanced training in how to *share* their faith, *follow-up* new believers and *encourage* growing Christians.

COURSE FORMAT AND CONTENT

The course format is designed around a participatory learning process which requires a minimum of assigned homework.

Each **Student's Kit** includes:

- *A Closer Walk with God* (Student Bible Study Guide, IEA/Word)
- A *Spiritual Journal* - (Quarterly Refill IEA/Word)
- 2 sample witnessing tracts
- A scripture memory verse card holder
- Covenant Card

Each **Leader's Kit** includes:

- *Teacher's Preparation Cassettes*
- *A Closer Walk with God* (Leader's Guide)
- *A Closer Walk with God* (Student Bible Study Guide)
- *Everyday Evangelism* (resource reading)
- *If You Love Me* (resource reading)
- A *Spiritual Journal* - Suede Jacket Edition
- *Time Alone With God* (*If You Love Me* video #2 and brochure)
- 11 **audio-witness tracts** (cassettes) entitled *Assured Of Heaven*
- A sample witnessing tract
- A scripture memory verse card holder
- Art Slick (for class enlistment)
- Covenant Card

Note:
The *Assured of Heaven* audio-witness tract cassettes in your Leader's Kit are designed for use during the evangelism training segment of the course. There are 10 of these cassettes included in this kit to be distributed to your students at that time. If you enlist more than 10 class members, please order additional cassettes using the order form in your Student Bible Study Guide (see pre-addressed post card).

Introduction

Note:
An enriching *video resource* is available to you as a group leader. These four additional video sessions are optional. They are based on the book *If You Love Me* (see brochure). We recommend that you use these tapes for your personal spiritual preparation and for additional teaching illustrations. They are designed to *supplement*, not replace, your own personal illustrations in teaching. As the group leader, you are God's person to *teach* and *model* the exciting message and lifestyle of this curriculum. In many respects, you will find that the course basically teaches itself as you follow the suggestions included in this guide. Your foremost responsibility will be to *pray, read*, and come fully *prepared* to minister out of the spiritual *overflow* of your own walk with God.

The subjects included in this inspiring series are listed below.

If You Love Me (IEA/Word)
Billie Hanks Jr.

Message 1: *If You Love Me, Keep My Commandments* (55:21)
 – Receiving Christ
 – Walking in Christ
 – Hearing God's Word
*Message 2: *Time Alone with God* (52:00)
 – Jesus' Example
 – Let's Get Started in the *Quiet Time*
 – The Lord Planned Ahead
 * This devotional session teaches the use of the *Spiritual Journal*, and is already *included* in your Leader's Kit;
Message 3: *The Secret of Godliness* (52:30)
 – Fellowship with God
 – Prayers of Adoration
Message 4: *Adventures in Prayer, Part 1* (52:32)
 – Prayers of Petition
 – Prayers of Confession
Message 5: *Adventures in Prayer, Part 2* (52:24)
 – Prayers of Thanksgiving
 – Prayers of Intercession

TEACHING THE COURSE

A Closer Walk with God includes 5 Sections, which are taught in 13 Sessions. Each session is indicated by this sign – $\boxed{1}$.

The course has been especially designed for ease of instruction. Using its special format, your best ministry will come from leading your group as an *encourager* and *expeditor*. Much of the content is actually taught through *audible* reading. In this approach, you simply ask one of your class members to read a paragraph in the curriculum, then you make additional comments *illustrating* each point.

You may choose to do all of the audible reading yourself or involve class members in the reading process. If so, we recommend that you read the scriptures in unison. Reading skills will differ, and each class will have its own personality, so you must judge whether or not to use this approach.

In your sessions you will also "walk" your class members through the *Spiritual Journal*, paragraph by paragraph, explaining the blanks to be filled in during one's devotional experience.

Many helpful background insights will be provided by your preparatory reading assignments, but you can also expect the Holy Spirit to give you and your group rich new understanding as the scripture passages are read and discussed in each class period.

In each session, you will need to illustrate selected points of emphasis in the curriculum. To maximize your time, suggested illustrations have been provided. Please do not feel bound by these suggestions. They may not be the best choice for the specific needs of your class. Secondly, time may not allow you to use all the illustrations provided.

At the end of each session, a weekly *inspirational assignment* is provided. To encourage full participation, we recommend that you present the *Personal Spiritual Covenant* card. This presentation is made just *before* you give the first homework assignment. Be sure the

Introduction

covenant is carefully explained and presented in a spirit of expectation and sincerity.

Remind the class that spiritual *consistency* is our primary objective, and people tend to *complete* what they plan ahead to accomplish.

Note: *Personal Spiritual Covenant* cards are included with your course materials.

TIME FACTOR

Since your people will already be attending worship services, the only additional time required for the weekly assignments will be spent in having a daily *Quiet Time* and memorizing *one* new verse each week.

Each of the sessions, $\boxed{1}$ is timed for 45 minutes. If your required schedule is different from that, simply adjust as needed by shortening or lengthening each session. Adequate time is provided in the schedule to allow for stimulating group discussion.

The Student and Leader's Guides are designed for 13 sessions; however, the material can be taught in 7 weeks by simply adding 30 minutes to the class teaching time in Sessions 1 – 12, and covering *two* weekly Study Guide sessions by combining small group activities and homework assignments.

AT THE CONCLUSION OF THE COURSE

One of the spiritual objectives of this course is to help churches discover and develop potential **Disciplers** who feel led to serve in the areas of evangelistic outreach, follow-up, and new member assimilation. Those who become spiritually motivated through the *vision of multiplication* will be prime candidates for your church's ongoing discipling ministry.

As the course nears its conclusion, you can prayerfully recruit your interested members to be trained in the *A Call to Joy* follow-up course, so they will be prepared to develop Christ-centered friendships with new members. (Coordinate these plans with your church's pastor or minister of discipleship or assimilation, as you look toward the graduation of your class).

Hopefully, your class members will feel led to enlist in another elective class in *The Christian Essentials Series*. If this is true, they will automatically be encouraged to continue using their journals. Your spiritual goal is to help them enjoy their devotional practice so it will be their *lifestyle*.

To solidify this commitment in Session 12, the class will be reminded to order their Journal Refills using the pre-addressed post card in their *Study Guides*. At this time, they will also be asked to evaluate the course and offer their suggestions for our curriculum development team.

ADDITIONAL RESOURCE MATERIAL INCLUDED IN YOUR LEADER'S GUIDE

PREPARATORY READING FOR TEACHING SECTION 3
The Making of a Disciple

Appendix A — *The Public and Private Ministry of Jesus*

This resource material distinguishes between *teaching* and *training*, then suggests some basic *presuppositions* for an effective discipling ministry based upon Jesus' pattern. It is designed to help increase your understanding of *Spiritual Multiplication* as you prepare to teach.

Appendix B — *Spiritual Friendship with New Christians*

Appendix C — *The Burden of My Heart*

PREPARATORY READING FOR TEACHING SECTION 4
Sharing the Truth in Love

Appendix D — *Sharing Christ Naturally* (offers helpful suggestions on teaching the three sessions on evangelism)

Appendix E — *Personal Conversion Story* (Form)

PREPARATORY READING FOR TEACHING SECTION 5
Living By Faith

Appendix F — *The Indwelling Christ* (The Key to Victory!)

PREPARATORY READING FOR TEACHING SECTIONS 1 – 5

Appendix G — *Lesson Illustrations* (selected to supplement your group reading)

Note: If your church is planning to offer *A Closer Walk with God* in a traditional Sunday School setting with an opening assembly, we suggest that you teach from your resource reading during that period of time.

SESSION 1

"Seek ye out of the book of the Lord and read"
(ISAIAH 34:16A, KJV).

PURPOSE

A. In this session you will seek to lead each of your class members to begin taking *effective notes* during Bible study and worship services. This discipline will require no extra time but will greatly *increase* personal retention of the spiritual lessons and insights being learned.

B. *Challenge* — Our times of worship and personal Bible reading are the most important hours of the week; that's why we need to *retain* and *apply* what God teaches us.

PREPARATION

A. Carefully read or listen to the following:
   • Teacher's Preparation Cassette — Overview and Session 1
   • *Study Guide*, pages 1-5, up to "II" (Student Book)
   • The *Spiritual Journal*, pages 2-3, 46-47
   • *If You Love Me*, chapters 1&2

B. Become familiar with the following presentation, making any additional personal teaching notes in the margins of your *Study Guide*. Seek to be spiritually ready to lead your group with a minimum amount of reference to this Guide. Pray that the Lord will enable you to teach out of the overflow of your personal time spent with Him.

PRESENTATION

A. Course overview (5-10 minutes).
   • Welcome class members to the rewarding experience of learning how to have a closer walk with God.
   • Explain the course format: leader or group reading and minimal homework assignments.

Session 1 9

- Open with prayer, asking God to teach each class member new and life-changing truths from His Word (**PSALM 119:18**).

B. Group Reading — Begin by audibly reading the *Study Guide* "Introduction," pages 1-2, followed by the *Spiritual Journal*, "A Personal Word," pages 2-3 (15-20 minutes). Discuss and emphasize any truth you feel to be of special importance.

C. *Study Guide* — "We Hear God's Word for Faith," pages 4-5 (group reading, 15-20 minutes). Supplement the group reading by using your choice of selected illustrations from the *Leader's Guide*, Appendix G.
- First, read page 3 and take time to teach the *fingers* of:

THE WORD OF GOD – HAND ILLUSTRATION

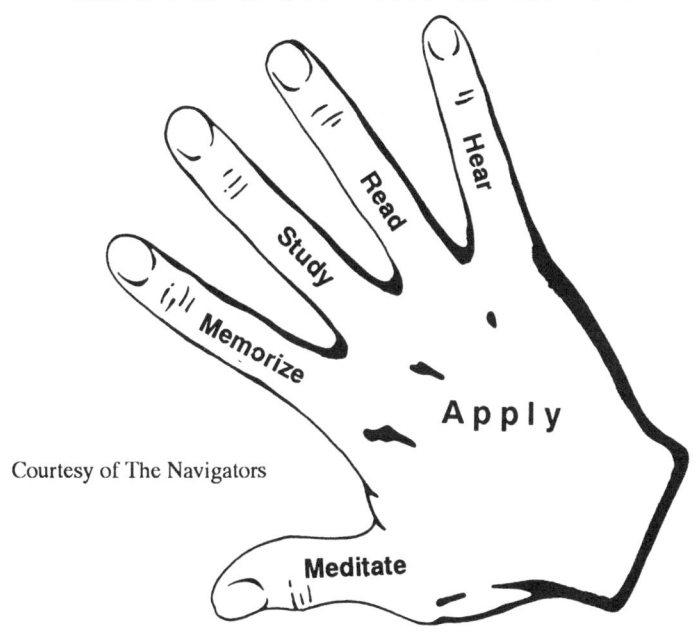

Hear, Read, Study, Memorize, Apply, Meditate

Courtesy of The Navigators

- In teaching the **Hand Illustration**, make the following observations:
    (1) Your little finger is the weakest on your hand, but it is still very important. *Hearing* is the easiest of the spiritual disciplines, but it is also very important.

(2) Each larger finger on your hand is progressively stronger. Correlating each new spiritual discipline is progressively harder and increasingly beneficial in your growth as a Christian.

Example:
To illustrate this point, ask the class to hold their Bibles with their thumbs and little fingers. Ask how secure they would feel going into battle against Satan holding a sword with this *one finger grip!* Next, call out the name of each finger (hear, read, study, memorize, meditate) and ask them to add one additional finger to their grip as you call them out. Their *grip* will begin to feel secure. Remind them that "...*we wrestle not against flesh and blood...but, against the spiritual forces of evil in the heavenly realms*"(EPHESIANS 6:12, NIV). Therefore, a good grip on God's word is *essential* for battle. In closing, write the word "Apply" in the center of the hand, and quote JAMES 1:22.

Note: *Witnessing* is not listed on the **Hand Illustration** because it is a spiritual *by-product* of the intake that comes from these six other disciplines.

• Continue reading "A-F" on pages 4&5, making additional comments as you feel led.

Blanks:
Psychologists tell us that after 72 hours we normally **remember:**
Only about 10% of what we **hear**.
Only about 30% of what we **read**.
About 50% of what we **hear** and **read**.
About 90% of what we **hear**, **read**, and **do**!
Discuss these blanks on an experiential level.

• Under "C" teach the class the *"Yes, Lord, Yes!"* illustration from *If You Love Me*, pages 11&12 (Fill in the blank).
• Under "D" explain that God does *not* tell us to do one thing and then do something else Himself. He gives insight and spiritual pearls to those who know how to *value* knowledge and truth. Illustrate this thought and ask your class to fill in the blank as a brief reminder of your illustration.

Session 1   11

- Under "E" read and explain the Sermon Notes section of the *Spiritual Journal* (pages 46&47) and the blanks on pages 48-87.
- If you are running short of time, briefly *summarize* "F" by emphasizing the *four* practical suggestions.
- Make the *Spiritual Covenant Card* presentation to each class member.

ASSIGNMENT AND CLOSING (3-5 minutes). Carefully explain each assignment, making sure that everyone understands what is expected. Emphasize the fact that the time required for *daily success* is minimal, so everyone should do well.

ASSIGNMENTS:

A. Take notes during Bible study and worship services, using your *Spiritual Journal*. (**Note**: If your class is conducted *before* a worship service, ask the group members to begin taking notes in the upcoming service).

B. Give each group member a memory verse holder, and ask them to remove their memory verse card for the week (see perforated verse cards). Memorize **ROMANS 3:23**, remembering to quote the reference both *before* and *after* the verse. Practice quoting the verse several times each day. (Example: "**ROMANS 3:23**—For all have sinned, and come short of the glory of God—**ROMANS 3:23**" [KJV]).

C. Be prepared to share *Quiet Time* highlights, scripture verse, and note-taking insights next week.

Close by selecting one class member to lead in prayer.

SESSION 2

"Morning by morning, O Lord, You hear my voice; morning by morning I lay my requests before You and wait in expectation" (PSALM 5:3, NIV).

PURPOSE

A. This session is designed to equip and motivate each of your class members to begin or continue having a consistent *daily Quiet Time.*

B. *Challenge* — Out of 1,440 daily minutes, let's dedicate 15 special minutes back to the Lord at the beginning of each day!

PREPARATION

A. Prayerfully re-read your *Study Guide*, pages 1&2, noting the subjects you will want to briefly review with your class.

B. Read, listen to, or view the following:
  • Teacher's Preparation Cassette — Session 2
  • *Study Guide*, pages 5-10, all of "II"
  • View the video, *Time Alone With God*
  • The *Spiritual Journal*, pages 6-8, 20&21
  • *If You Love Me*, chapters 3&4. Supplement the group reading by using your choice of selected illustrations from the *Leader's Guide*, Appendix G.

C. Carefully review the following presentation, writing your own teaching notes in the margins of your *Study Guide*.

PRESENTATION

A. *Accountability* — Divide your group into pairs, (if practical, men with men, women with women). This period is designed for group members to enjoy exchanging favorite *insights* from sermon, personal Bible study, or Sunday School notes, so ask your class members to do this using their *Spiritual Journals*. Next, ask them to practice quoting the scripture memory verse of the week to each other (ROMANS 3:23) (7-10 minutes).

Session 2   13

B. *Study Guide* — "We Read God's Word for Fellowship," pages 5-10 (group reading, 15-20 minutes).
 • Begin by briefly reviewing last weeks *Study Guide* highlights.
 • Go around the circle or row by row, asking class members to each read a paragraph or section in the outline on these pages (five sections included, with a primary emphasis on "C").
 • Be sure that the Scriptures are read with their references, and that any **boldface** words are emphasized.
 Note: When possible, share fresh and meaningful illustrations from your *own* life and ministry. A real but brief testimony is powerful!

C. *Spiritual Journal,* "How to Use the *Quiet Time* Section" (10-15 minutes).
 • Prayerfully present the *Quiet Time* section of the journal, page 6&7 (group reading), noting the actual blanks on pages 20-21.
 • Briefly explain page 8. Point out that this week's memory verse should be written on the line at the *top* of page 20. New verses are to be *added* and *reviewed* as demonstrated on page 8.
 • Ask if any members of your class are already having a *Quiet Time*. If anyone is, ask him/her to share the benefits.

ASSIGNMENT AND CLOSING (3-5 minutes)

A. Continue notetaking in *worship services* and other Bible study opportunities. Remember, we are seeking to develop a *consistent lifestyle* of fellowship with God.

B. Start having a daily *Quiet Time* and record new insights in your *Spiritual Journal.* Lead the class in a prayer of commitment, dedicating 10-15 minutes to God at the beginning of each day during the remaining weeks of this course. Tell them not to be discouraged if they are providentially hindered for honorable reasons known to God, but to plan ahead for victory!

C. Memorize **ROMANS 6:23**. Remind them again to learn each new verse by repeating the reference *before* and *after* the scripture.

D. Be prepared to share *Quiet Time* highlights, scripture verses, and notetaking insights next week.

Write out this week's new verse at the top of page 20. Next, write the reference **ROMANS 3:23** on the first line under "Scripture Memory Review." *Check off* each day as you *learn* this week's new verse and review the previous one.

> **Note:** Give each group member one copy of the printed witnessing tract. Ask them to read the tract at home and then prayerfully give it to someone during the week!

Close by asking *two* of the participants to pray, one man and one woman.

SESSION 3

"For everything that was written in the past was written to teach us, so that through endurance and the encouragement of the Scriptures we might have hope" (ROMANS 15:4, NIV).

PURPOSE

A. In this session, you will lead your class toward a *lifestyle* of Bible study and scripture memory!

B. ***Challenge*** — Good Bible study requires the *desire* to learn, and scripture memory requires the *desire* to live effectively; let's ask God for a deep hunger and *desire* for both.

PREPARATION

A. Prayerfully re-read your *Study Guide*, pages 3-10, noting the subjects you will want to briefly *review* with your group.

B. Read or listen to the following:
   - Teacher's Preparation Cassette — Session 3
   - *Study Guide*, pages 10-14, all of "III" and "IV"
   - *If You Love Me*, chapter 5

C. Study the outline below, making additional notes from your reading and personal experience; be ready to teach these two new sections.

PRESENTATION

A. *Study Guide* — "We Study God's Word for Knowledge," pages 10-11 (group reading, 10-15 minutes). Supplement the group reading by using your choice of selected illustrations from the *Leader's Guide*, Appendix G.
   - Begin by briefly reviewing last weeks *Study Guide* highlights.
   - Supplement and explain the verses as needed, noting the importance of gaining "knowledge" and "understanding" through consistent Bible study.
   - Explain *why* an effective personal witness typically requires a

basic knowledge of several key verses on salvation. Emphasize the fact that the verses presently being *memorized* will help each class member feel confident in presenting the "good news" about Jesus Christ.

"... Always be prepared to give an answer to everyone who asks you to give the reason for the hope that you have"
(1 PETER 3:15, NIV).

• Lead a brief discussion on the *seven* practical suggestions given in "Section C".

B. *Accountability* — Divide into pairs and review your current memory verses, *Quiet Time* insights, and sermon notes (7-10 minutes).

C. *Study Guide* — "We Memorize God's Word for Successful Living," pages 11-14 (group reading, 20-25 minutes).
• Read and briefly discuss Section IV. Emphasize key points and major on making scripture memory a normal part of daily life. Suggest available moments that can be used for scripture memory. **Examples:** Waiting for appointments, exercising, driving, dressing, etc.
• Focus on the great devotional verses in Item "C" (page 13).

ASSIGNMENT AND CLOSING (3-5 minutes)

A. Continue *notetaking* in worship services and Bible studies.

B. Continue building consistency in your daily *Quiet Times*.

C. Memorize **HEBREWS 9:27**, making this week's new *Spiritual Journal* entry. Review previous memory verses, placing *check marks* in the daily boxes. (Find out how many of your class members normally *pray* at meals. As an assignment, ask them to begin quoting their new memory verse of the week after each grace is offered. This will allow for 21 opportunities to learn the new verse each week)!

D. Be prepared to share *Quiet Time* highlights, scripture verses, and note-taking insights next week.

Close in group prayer, asking two or three to offer *sentence* prayers.

SESSION 4

"Be still and know that I am God"
(PSALM 46:10a, NKJV).

PURPOSE

A. In this session you will prayerfully seek to show the importance of spiritual *meditation* and *application*.

B. *Challenge* — In a busy world, let's plan to carve some islands in our days for *quiet reflection* and *fellowship* with Christ!

PREPARATION

A. Re-read your *Study Guide*, pages 1-13, carefully jotting down what you want to *review* from your session on *hearing, reading, studying,* and *memorizing* God's Word. Pray that the entire class will be led to understand that spiritual growth produces true *joy* and inner *fulfillment*.

B. Read or listen to the following:
 • Teacher's Preparation Cassette — Session 4
 • *Study Guide*, pages 14-16, all of "V" and "VI"
 • *If You Love Me*, chapter 11

C. Read through the following presentation, writing additional notes in the margins of your *Study Guide*. Be prepared to lead a meaningful discussion on the importance of meditating on scripture and applying it in daily life.

PRESENTATION

A. *Study Guide* — "We Meditate on God's Word for Understanding," pages 14-16 (group reading by paragraphs and sections, 12-15 minutes). Supplement the group reading by using your choice of selected illustrations from the *Leader's Guide*, Appendix G.
 • Begin by briefly reviewing last weeks *Study Guide* highlights.

- Discuss the definition for Christian meditation. It could be defined as "prayerfully *reflecting* on God's Word so we can be *conformed* to Christ-likeness in attitude and character." Richard Foster defines meditation as "the ability to *hear* God's voice and *obey* His word" (*Celebration of Discipline*, page 17). We are nourished by the Word of God spiritually as we build our lives around it and repeatedly *focus* on its truth. A sincere desire for *obedience* to God's Word is the primary ingredient for successful Christian meditation.
- Ask your group to read through this section, point by point ("A" through "G" under "V"). Explain what you feel to be most important about each statement and verse of scripture.
- Note that *meditation* prepares our hearts for close communion with God! We do not *run* into His presence; we approach Him quietly with hearts prepared to *listen* and *respond* in faith.

B. *Accountability* — Divide your group into pairs and review memory verses, new *Quiet Time* insights, and sermon notes (10 minutes).

C. *Study Guide* — "We Apply God's Word for Continued Growth," page 16, and page 6 in the *Spiritual Journal* (group reading, 20-25 minutes).
- Read through the three parts of item "VI" and discuss as desired. Emphasize D. L. Moody's excellent statement and the author's quote on page 38 of *If You Love Me*.
- Turn to the *Spiritual Journal*, page 6, and briefly review that page. Emphasize items 2 and 4, noting the importance of making personal applications during *Quiet Times*. In addition to the five parts of the **SPACE** acrostic you can add these four:
  — Is there a . . . **Prayer for me to** *pray*?
  Error for me to *avoid*?
  Truth for me to *believe*?
  Something worthy of *praise*?
  — This makes our acrostic **SPACE PETS** (Richard Warren, *Dynamic Bible Study Methods*, page 35).
  — When your class members write their devotional applications, they should be *personal, practical, possible,* and *provable*. (Provable, as we use it, means something for which you can

Session 4

hold yourself *accountable*).

ASSIGNMENT AND CLOSING (3-5 minutes)

A. Continue notetaking and daily *Quiet Times*, using your journal.

B. During the coming week, purpose to meditate on *one* especially meaningful *truth* which you hear, read, or memorize from God's Word.

C. Memorize **ROMANS 5:8** and review the previous three verses. Be sure to *check off* the journal squares as you review each day.

D. Be prepared to share *Quiet Time* highlights, scripture verses, and note-taking insights next week.

Close by singing a brief chorus of dedication or praise, or by praying as you feel led.

Examples:
> *God Is So Good*
> *Father I Adore You*
> *I Have Decided To Follow Jesus*

SESSION 5

"Call to Me, and I will answer you, and show you great and mighty things, which you do not know" (JEREMIAH 33:3, NKJV).

PURPOSE

A. In this session, you will be seeking to communicate the *true spirit* of prayer. Like love, it must not be legalistic!

B. *Challenge* — Do we really understand that our lives and ministries will rise no higher than our commitment to believing prayer?

PREPARATION

A. Using your *Study Guide*, pages 14-16, "V and VI", note the areas you want to review on *meditation* and *application*.

B. Read or listen to the following:
   • Teacher's Preparation Cassette — Session 5
   • *Study Guide*, pages 17-19 (The Prayer – Hand Illustration and Sections I, II, and III)
   • The *Spiritual Journal*, pages 9-13
   • *If You Love Me*, chapters 6&7

C. Read through the following presentation. Prepare to lead a meaningful *discussion* on answered prayer, soliciting brief *testimonies* from your group. Explain that all prayer is answered — but sometimes with *no*, sometimes with *yes,* and sometimes with *wait!*

PRESENTATION

A. *Accountability* — Divide into pairs and *review* all memory verses (seek to be word-perfect, quoting references before and after each verse); exchange *Quiet Time* insights and personal applications; next, discuss insights learned from sermon notes (10-12 minutes).

Session 5   21

B. *Study Guide* — "Conversing with God through Prayer, Experiencing God's Love and Fellowship through Prayer, and Affecting the Lives of Others through Prayer," pages 17-19, "I, II, and III" (group reading, 15-20 minutes).
   • Begin by briefly reviewing last weeks *Study Guide* highlights.
   • Guide your group through:

THE PRAYER – HAND ILLUSTRATION
(page 17)

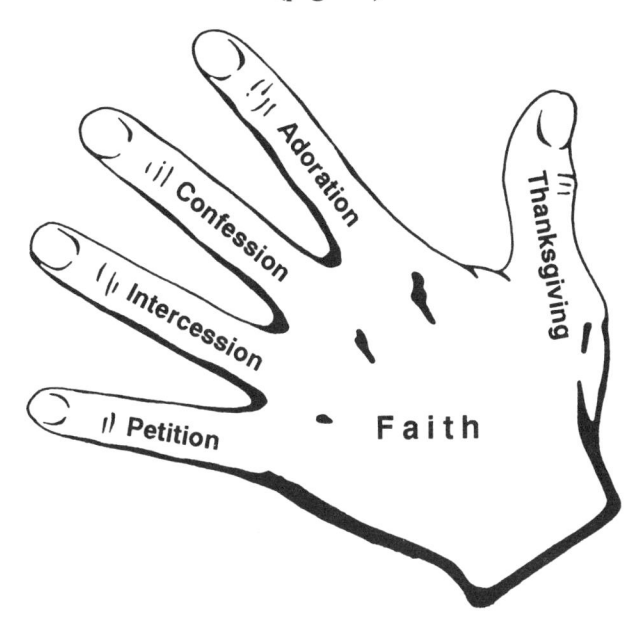

[Illustration of a hand with fingers labeled: Adoration, Confession, Intercession, Petition, Thanksgiving, and palm labeled Faith]

Note: Emphasize the fact that our *heart attitude* is to be one of *thanksgiving*, and this will naturally affect every area of our experience in prayer.
   • Briefly discuss how we can *combine* our Bible reading with prayer to enhance our daily *Quiet Times*.
   Example: As you read, stop and pray specifically about needs, promises, or ministry opportunities as the Holy Spirit brings them to your attention.

C. *Spiritual Journal*, page 9 — "Prayers of Adoration," (group reading, 10 minutes).

- Note that the greatest and highest form of prayer is ADORATION because in it we ask absolutely nothing for *ourselves* and every thought is directed toward God—praising Him for *who* He is!
- Read and discuss page 9 in the *Spiritual Journal*, and ask one member of your group to slowly read **1 CHRONICLES 29:11-13** and other selected verses. Use this opportunity to vividly demonstrate the unique qualities of adoration. In order for your group to move beyond petition, confession, and intercession, they will need to *consciously* offer adoration at first, but with experience, this will come naturally.

D. If time allows, seek to learn how *consistent* the group is being with their spiritual disciplines. Ask those who are enjoying consistent *success* to share their positive experience.

ASSIGNMENT AND CLOSING (5-10 minutes)

A. Continue notetaking, daily *Quiet Times*, meditation on scripture, and prayer. Remember to keep your *Spiritual Journal* with your Bible and use it regularly.

B. Memorize **EPHESIANS 2:8-9** and review your four previous verses.

C. Be prepared to share *Quiet Time* highlights, notetaking insights, and scripture verses next week.

D. Rejoice in the Lord and plan to be consistent in your daily fellowship with Him. The Psalmist said,

"May my meditation be sweet to Him; I will be glad in the Lord"
(PSALM 104:34, NKJV).

Focus on the *person* of Christ, then close by asking group members to offer brief *one-sentence prayers of adoration*.

Example:
"Lord, you are _____ to me!"

SESSION 6

"Therefore I say to you, all things for which you pray and ask, believe that you have received them, and they shall be granted you"
(MARK 11:24, NASB).

PURPOSE

A. In this session, your class members will be introduced to *four* of the five types of prayer taught in the Bible.

B. *Challenge* — If prayer is of vital importance to God, it should be of vital importance to us — so let's examine our priorities!

PREPARATION

A. Using your *Study Guide,* pages 17-19," I, II, and III", prayerfully select what to *review* from your previous material. Encourage your group members to establish new *patterns in prayer.*

B. Read or listen to the following:
 • Teacher's Preparation Cassette — Session 6
 • *Study Guide,* pages 19-20, concentrating on "V"
 • The *Spiritual Journal,* pages 9-19
 • *If You Love Me,* chapters 8-10 (**Note** — this week's reading is *longer* than usual, so you will need to be selective in the number of illustrations which you use).

C. Read through the following presentation, writing notes on what you want to emphasize when teaching these four important classifications of prayer — *confession, intercession, petition,* and *thanksgiving.*

PRESENTATION

A. *Accountability* — Divide your group into pairs, then ask them to review their five memory verses. Next, lead them to exchange favorite *Quiet Time* insights and sermon notes. In conclusion, ask each pair to briefly discuss their favorite single aspect of the course (10 minutes).

B. *Study Guide* — "Prayer" (remainder of the section), pages 19-20 (group reading, 25 minutes). Supplement the group reading by using your choice of selected illustrations from the *Leader's Guide*, Appendix G.
- Begin by briefly reviewing last weeks *Study Guide* highlights.
- Briefly *review* the Prayer-Hand Illustration, naming each of the five approaches being studied.
- *Read* and *discuss* (teaching the proper use of the *Spiritual Journal*)
  — Prayers of **Petition**, *Spiritual Journal*, pages 10, 18-19
  — Prayers of **Confession**, *Spiritual Journal*, page 11
  — Prayers of **Thanksgiving**, *Spiritual Journal*, page 12
  — Prayers of **Intercession**, *Spiritual Journal*, pages 13-17
  Discuss why a "No!" can be just as important as a "Yes!"

C. Review and Evaluation: You are now completing a very important part of the course, so stop to *briefly discuss* how daily spiritual intake affects *every* area of one's life (2-5 minutes).

ASSIGNMENT AND CLOSING (3-5 minutes)

A. Continue your spiritual disciplines—sermon notetaking, daily *Quiet Times*, and journaling, using each section provided.

B. Memorize JOHN 1:12 and review the previous *five* verses. Check off the appropriate squares on your *Quiet Time* page as you complete this week's assignment.

C. Be prepared to share *Quiet Time* highlights, scripture verses, and notetaking insights next week.

D. List the names of *friends* and their *specific* needs (*Spiritual Journal*, pages 14-17). Next, write this week's personal prayer requests on pages 18-19.

Close by asking *two* pre-selected persons to pray.

SESSION 7

"Follow my example as I follow the example of Christ"
(1 CORINTHIANS 11:1, NCV).

PURPOSE

A. In this session, you will be introducing your class to the very *heart* of our Lord's earthly ministry.

B. **Challenge** — Let's commit ourselves to live with a true sense of destiny, investing in something that will last forever – people!

PREPARATION

A. Look back over pages 1-20 in your *Study Guide* and decide which portions of the material you would like to review with the class. Remember that the spiritual goal of this course is real and lasting change, so review is important.

B. Read or listen to the following:
  • Teacher's Preparation Cassette — Session 7
  • *Study Guide*, pages 21-25, stopping at "The First Century Vision for Making Disciples"
  • *Leader's Guide*, Appendix A — "The Public and Private Ministry of Jesus"
  • *Everyday Evangelism*, chapters 1&2 for your personal enrichment

C. Read through the presentation below, and write your teaching notes in the margins of your *Study Guide*. The biblical emphasis for Section 3 is discipleship.
  • Think about the two foundational principles (page 21). Every disciple should be sharing his *witness* with others out of the spiritual *overflow* of his daily fellowship with Christ.
  • Jesus' method of *training* His followers is described in the four gospels and is best seen in His *example*. His transferable methods are also clearly seen in the lives of first century Christian leaders.

- Appendix A in the *Leader's Guide* provides additional insight into the Lord's methods of ministry. It then suggests some *presuppositions* for your own life and ministry as a teacher.

PRESENTATION

A. *Accountability* — Divide your group into pairs; exchange new insights, quote current memory verses, and share one personal prayer request (7-10 minutes).

B. *Study Guide* — "Two Foundational Principles" (page 21); briefly explain and illustrate these points, then lead the group to repeat them in unison.
- Begin by briefly reviewing last weeks *Study Guide* highlights.
- Discuss the fact that early Christians owned no books, tapes, or Bibles, yet they impacted their world through the *quality* of their lives (3-5 minutes).

C. *Study Guide* — "Jesus' Method of Training His Followers," pages 21-25 (group reading, 25-30 minutes).
- Carefully move through the four points under "Jesus demonstrated His Training Method . . . "; add to your discussion an illustration on the difference between *teaching* and *training* (*Leader's Guide,* Appendix A).
- Discuss how Jesus taught and trained His disciples to be spiritual reproducers. Note the ways He accomplished this (pages 21-22, including the illustration).
- Briefly present the suggested presuppositions for ministry based on Jesus' example (*Leader's Guide,* Appendix A) after II B.
- Conclude by reading about the ministries of Barnabas, Paul, Peter, and John (pages 23-25). Stop and emphasize *key* words and sentences that demonstrate:

  — *Early Church follow-up*
  — *The importance of apprenticeship*
  — *The place of friendship in discipling*

Session 7

ASSIGNMENT AND CLOSING: (3-5 minutes)

A. Continue daily *Quiet Times* and sermon notetaking.

B. Memorize ROMANS 10:9-10 and review the previous six verses, checking off the appropriate boxes on the *Quiet Time* page of your *Spiritual Journal*.

C. Be prepared to share *Quiet Time* highlights, scripture verses, and notetaking insights next week.

D. Make new entries in your *Spiritual Journal* as you learn to enjoy all five kinds of prayer. Come prepared to tell about one very *specific answer* from the Intercessory Prayer Section of your journal.

Example:
—*A relationship healed*
—*A need met*
—*A circumstance changed*

> **Note:** Give each group member one copy of the printed witnessing tract. Ask each of them to read the tract at home and then prayerfully give it to someone during the week!

Lead in a closing prayer, celebrating what God is doing in each participant's life!

SESSION 8

"Then He appointed twelve, that they might be with Him and He might send them out to preach" (MARK 3:14, NASB).

PURPOSE

A. In this session, you will prayerfully seek to show your class the *fastest* and most *effective* way to reach our world for Christ!

B. *Challenge* — May God use those in our group to help *win, nurture,* and *train* this generation – as we prepare for the second coming.

PREPARATION

A. Look back over pages 21-25 in your *Study Guide* and decide which portions of the material you would like to review with the class.

B. Read or listen to the following:
   - Teacher's Preparation Cassette — Session 8
   - *Study Guide,* pages 25-29, Sections III & IV, taking special note of the illustration on "The Power of Spiritual Multiplication"
   - *Leader's Guide,* Appendix B—"Spiritual Friendship with New Christians"
   - *Everyday Evangelism,* chapters 6&7 for your personal enrichment

PRESENTATION

A. *Study Guide* — "The First Century Vision for Making Disciples," all four points, pages 25-26 (group reading, 15 minutes). Supplement the group reading by using your choice of selected illustrations from the *Leader's Guide,* Appendix G.
   - Begin by briefly reviewing last week's *Study Guide* highlights.
   - Ask one person to read each of the numbered paragraphs under point "A"; comment briefly on each paragraph.
   - Emphasize MARK 3:14 and the "personal relationship" approach to ministry that we were given to follow.

Session 8   29

- Ask one of your class members to read JOHN 21:15-17. Discuss the fact that our love for Christ is demonstrated by the quality of *follow-up* and *nurture* which we provide for His people. To love Him is to love those whom He loves!

B. *Study Guide* — "The Power of Spiritual Multiplication," pages 27-29 (storytelling format, 15 - 20 minutes).
- Develop and tell an "exaggerated story "about two aggressive witnesses named *Charlie* and *Sam*. **Example:** Charlie works for a major company and has the ability to talk and sell with ease. He wins *one* person to Christ *every week*. Sam is even more unusual – he wins *one* person to Christ *every day!* Picture him as a star athlete, with a warm, sincere personality and lots of energy, etc. Next, select a class member and let him be your example of spiritual multiplication. Have some fun picturing him as a normal person who only wins *one* person to Christ *each year*. Next, point out how significantly the numbers increase as your class member begins to multiply spiritually for only ten years! Before completing the illustration, re-emphasize the fact that your class member only *personally reached one* for Christ per year. This is what makes spiritual multiplication so workable in everyday life.
- Emphasize this lesson by briefly reading Section "C" (page 29) *twice!* Challenge your group members to think in terms of living *every new year* with the goal of praying with at least *one* person to receive Christ, and then sharing all they know about growing, until the one they have helped is helping another. This is how the early church *grew!*

C. *Accountability* — If time permits, divide your group into pairs; then ask them to recite ROMANS 10:9-10; exchange a new lesson learned from sermon notes, and share one new *Quiet Time* insight.

ASSIGNMENT AND CLOSING (5 minutes)

A. Continue daily *Quiet Times*, scripture memory, and notetaking.

B. Memorize JOHN 5:24 and continue to practice your seven previous verses. Remember to *review* after prayer at meal times. This will make the process easy and enjoyable!

C. Be sure to give thanks as prayers are answered! Continue using the Intercessory Prayer and Special Prayer pages (14-19) in your *Spiritual Journal.*

Explain this important verse:

"*Now this is the confidence that we have in Him, that if we ask anything according to His will, He hears us*" (1 JOHN 5:14, NKJV).

Close in prayer, focusing on the fact that it is God's *will* that none should perish, so we can *boldly* pray asking to become multiplying disciples!

SESSION 9

"And the things which you have heard from me in the presence of many witnesses, these entrust to faithful men, who will be able to teach others also" (2 TIMOTHY 2:2, NASB).

PURPOSE

A. In this session, you will be teaching the valuable ministry of personally investing in people.

B. *Challenge* —Let's dare to choose an *unselfish* lifestyle that will make a lasting difference in our world!

PREPARATION

A. Reread your *Study Guide*, pages 25-29, noting what you want to *review* in this session. We are continuing to study discipleship.

B. Read or listen to the following:
   • Teacher's Preparation Cassette — Session 9
   • The audio-witness tract (listen)
   • *Study Guide*, pages 29-36; focus on these three segments:
     — "Steps Toward a Discipling Ministry"
     — "How to Begin a Ministry of Personal Follow-up"
     — "How to Be a Disciple (Trainee)"
   • *Everyday Evangelism*, chapter 8 for your personal enrichment
   • *Leader's Guide*, Appendix C — "The Burden of My Heart"

PRESENTATION

A. Before teaching the *Study Guide*, briefly read and then explain 1 CORINTHIANS 3:10-14, focusing on the *follow-up* ministry of Apollos (v. 10) and those who were exhorted to build lasting spiritual qualities into the lives of others (3 minutes).

B. *Study Guide* — "Steps Toward a Discipling Ministry," pages 29-31 (group reading, 9-12 minutes). Supplement the group reading by using your choice of illustrations from the *Leader's Guide,* Appendix G.

- Begin by briefly reviewing last weeks *Study Guide* highlights.
- Discuss the fact that enjoying a good follow-up ministry requires building a *friendship* and investing personal *time*.
- Explain and illustrate the importance of seeking to live as a good *example* .
- Focus on point "D"; discuss the fact that assisting others should be a *natural* and *consistent* part of our lives.

C. *Study Guide* — "How to Begin a Ministry of Personal Follow-up," pages 32-35 (group reading, 9-12 minutes).

D. *Study Guide* — "How to Be a Disciple," pages 35-36 (group reading, 9-12 minutes).
- Most of your class members will not yet feel prepared to follow-up a new Christian or disciple a growing believer; however, many will *desire further training*. This segment basically teaches them how to proceed in that direction.
- Conclude with a strong *spiritual challenge* presenting this formula (Availability + Usability = Effective Ministry). Next, read the boxed *Insight*, and then close with a prayer of *personal commitment*.

ASSIGNMENT AND CLOSING (3-5 minutes)

A. Continue daily *Quiet Times* and sermon notetaking. Begin praying *daily* for the *opportunity* to witness. Meditate on the promise of **JOHN 16: 8-9**,
 "*And when He* [**the Holy Spirit**] *has come, He will convict the world of sin, and of righteousness, and of judgment: of sin, because they do not believe in Me*" (**NKJV**).

B. Memorize **JOHN 10:28-29** and *review* the eight verses already memorized.

C. Be prepared to share *Quiet Time* highlights, notetaking insights, and experiences using the *Assured of Heaven* audio-witness tract.

Session 9

In closing, explain the use of the audio-witness tract. Then invite two or three group members to lead in prayer, asking God to specifically *convict* their *unbelieving* friends or loved ones of their need for Christ! Distribute the cassettes to the group.

Assured Of Heaven
The Audio-Witness Tract

This is a straightforward presentation of the gospel, designed to confront non-believers with the facts about eternal life and eternal death. In a generation with many non-readers, God is using this approach as an excellent conversation builder. After the closing song, *Forgiven,* there is a brief closing comment.

Ask each class member to carefully listen to the presentation themselves before giving, loaning, or mailing it to a non-Christian friend. Encourage them to develop a lifestyle of evangelistic concern and witness, and always keep either printed or audio tracts available for personal ministry!

SESSION 10

"But you shall receive power when the Holy Spirit has come upon you; and you shall be witnesses to Me . . . to the end of the earth"
(ACTS 1:8, NKJV).

PURPOSE

A. In this session, you will have the joy of demonstrating how *easy* and *natural* sharing one's faith can be.

B. **Challenge** — Witnessing is the work of the *Holy Spirit* – so let's trust Him to give us the words we need for each new opportunity!

PREPARATION

A. As an overview, scan your *Study Guide*, pages 37-43, then determine what you want to emphasize during this exciting session on personal evangelism. The unified theme will be sharing Christ *naturally* as a lifestyle. We all enjoy talking about those we love, so the better we truly know the Lord, the easier it will be to witness.

B. Read or listen to the following:
   • Teacher's Preparation Cassette — Session 10
   • *Study Guide*, pages 37-38, Section I; memorize the definition for "sharing a word of truth".
   • *Everyday Evangelism*, chapter 3
   • *Leader's Guide*, Appendix D — "Sharing Christ Naturally"
   • Think back over your own witnessing opportunities; if possible, share a personal illustration which fits this week's subject.

C. Prepare to show your group members how to give a brief but effective witness. If you lack recent experience, *pray* for the opportunity to give your witness during the week.

Session 10 35

PRESENTATION

A. *Accountability* — Divide into pairs; spend the first few minutes exchanging *Quiet Time* insights, notetaking highlights, and telling about opportunities to loan or give away the audio-witness tract. Then briefly discuss 1 JOHN 2:3. What do the two "knows" mean in this verse? (8-10 minutes)

B. *Study Guide* — "Sharing a Word of Truth," pages 37-38 (group reading with *explanations, illustrations,* and *discussion*; using your choice of illustrations from the *Leader's Guide*, Appendix G, 25 - 30 minutes).
  • Begin by briefly reviewing last weeks *Study Guide* highlights.
  • Clarify the Word of Truth definition. Discuss the example of Andrew; then teach the curriculum, using your personal *Study Guide* notes.
  • Brainstorm the many everyday opportunities for *sharing a word of truth*. Ask for some specific examples:
  — *at school*
  — *with fellow workers*
  — *with new acquaintances*

C. **Call for a Commitment:** Challenge the group to be conscious of people's spiritual needs. Ask members to stop and specifically *pray* for opportunities to witness each day this week! (3-5 minutes).

ASSIGNMENT AND CLOSING (3-5 minutes)

A. Continue notetaking and daily *Quiet Times*. Pray each morning for the chance to *share a word of truth*, a tract, or the audio-witness tract.

B. Memorize 1 JOHN 2:3, while reviewing the previous ten verses.

Close by slowly reading ACTS 1:8 and MATTHEW 28:18-20 out loud – then pause and ask the group to say these words in unison. "... *I will be with you always* ..." Remind them that this week is included in that promise!

SESSION 11

"But sanctify Christ as Lord in your hearts, always being ready to make a defense to everyone who asks you to give an account for the hope that is in you, yet with gentleness and reverence"
(1 PETER 3:15, NKJV).

PURPOSE

A. This session is designed to encourage group members to consider, commit to *writing*, and personally tell their stories of conversion.

B. *Challenge* — Let's be prepared to witness, and ask God for divine opportunities to explain the plan of salvation.

PREPARATION

A. Scan your *Study Guide*, pages 38-43, prayerfully focusing on what you will reemphasize and teach from these important lessons. Note that giving a testimony often fits in between *sharing a word of truth* and *explaining the gospel*.

B. Prepare to distribute photocopies of the "My Personal Conversion Story" in this *Leader's Guide,* Appendix E.

C. Read or listen to the following:
   • Teacher's Preparation Cassette — Session 11
   • *Study Guide*, pages 38-39, Section II
   • *Everyday Evangelism*, chapter 4 (here the terminology used is "testimony")

D. Review the presentation below, writing your teaching notes in the margins of your *Study Guide*.

PRESENTATION

A. *Study Guide* — "Sharing My Personal Story," pages 38-39 (group reading, 20-25 minutes). Supplement the group reading by using your choice of illustrations from the *Leader's Guide*, Appendix G.

Session 11

- Begin by briefly reviewing last weeks *Study Guide* highlights.
- Study ACTS 26:1-28. Point out the pattern of Paul's story about what God did in his own life. Present the *personal story* definition, then illustrate it by leading the group to read LUKE 8:39. Note the *immediate obedience* of the witness described in this passage.
- Mention the *three* types of personal stories God has given us: (1) a conversion testimony, (2) a deeper commitment experience, and (3) the continual story of how He teaches us to live by faith.
- Ask, "How many of you already have a *conversion story?*" (this means the realization of a time when they placed their faith in Christ and personally trusted Him to: forgive their sin, take control of their life, and give them eternal life).
- Ask how many in the group have a *deeper commitment story* (a time when God specifically led them to make Him Lord over an unsurrendered area in their life). Explain that as we grow in our faith, it is the Holy Spirit's work to bring these *unsurrendered* areas to our attention.
- Prayer – "At the close of this session, we will have a time of prayer, and all of you who *want to* can privately make a new or deeper commitment to Christ. Some of you may need to begin witnessing, others may need assurance of salvation, and still others may need to become obedient in a specific area of attitude or behavior." (**Note:** As leader, this will be your *special opportunity* to help anyone in your group who still needs to make a personal commitment related to salvation). Ultimately, every child of God should have his or her own conversion story, and for some, this class session may be the *beginning!*
- Underscore the emphasis in "C"— we need to learn to be *sensitive* to the conditions and feelings of those with whom we share. We can always adapt our personal stories by focusing on the parts that *relate* most specifically to our listener's needs.

B. Move into groups of *two* and ask each person to share a *brief* story about what actually initiated his or her desire for a personal relationship with Jesus Christ (5-10 minutes).

C. Pre-select a member of your group to share his or her personal *conversion story* with the entire class (3-5 minutes).
- Restrict him or her to 3 minutes.
- Commend him or her for being *brief* and to the *point!*
- Emphasize the importance of sincerity and humility in witnessing.
- Next, ask several people to quickly *quote* their favorite memory verse. This should be fast, like "popcorn"!

(In addition, be sure someone quotes this week's new verse).

ASSIGNMENT AND CLOSING (3-5 minutes)

A. Continue *sermon notetaking* and daily *Quiet Times*.

B. Memorize 1 JOHN 5:13 and review all previous verses.

C. Distribute a copy of Appendix E from this *Leader's Guide* to each class member. During the week, briefly *write out* either your personal story of *conversion* or *deeper commitment* and be prepared to share it with your partner next week. (Explain the suggested format found in *Everyday Evangelism*, pages 62-64).

D. Be prepared to share *Quiet Time* highlights and memory verses next week.

If time permits, offer brief sentence prayers of *intercession* for non-Christian friends and family members.

Closing Quote: *"For you will be a witness for Him to all men of what you have seen and heard"* (ACTS 22:15, NASB).

SESSION 12

"Jesus said, I am the way, and the truth, and the life; no one comes to the Father, but through Me" (JOHN 14:6, NASB).

PURPOSE

A. This lesson is designed to teach your group members how to present God's *plan of salvation* in a simple and effective manner.

B. *Challenge*—Sadly, most Christians live and die never knowing the *joy* of leading anyone to the Savior – may our experience be totally different!

PREPARATION

A. Prayerfully determine what you would like to emphasize during this important lesson. Your subject will be explaining God's plan of salvation. The presentation in the *Study Guide* is self-explanatory, but as the leader, you will need to "walk" your class through this session. Be sure to practice using a good visual aid (an overhead projector, a chalk board, or a flipchart). This exciting approach to witnessing is especially easy to learn. It can be given by memory, in nearly any setting. For example, it can be drawn on a paper napkin, a scrap of paper, or even in the dirt.

B. Read or listen to the following:
- Teacher's Preparation Cassette — Session 12
- *Study Guide*, pages 39-43, Section III, including each ingredient of the gospel presentation
- *Everyday Evangelism*, chapter 5 (**Note:** this is another "walk through" type class session which utilizes several clear verses explaining salvation).
- Continue to review your memory verses, seeking to know them word-perfect. As the leader, you set the pace by your positive *example!*

C. As you prepare to teach this session, *practice* presenting the Bridge Illustration *three* times with believing friends, family members, or non-Christian friends. Experience has shown that God may give you the privilege of leading one of them to Christ even as you practice!

D. Learn the Bridge Illustration *so well* that you will not need any notes when teaching it to your class. Notice that there is *no group reading in this session*; you will simply focus on two activities — *accountability* and *teaching* the Bridge Illustration.

PRESENTATION

A. *Accountability* — Divide your group into pairs, then ask each team to carry out the following activities: first, exchange one new *insight* from the past week's *Quiet Times*; second, recite the new memory verse; third, briefly review The Bridge Illustration memory verses; fourth, ask the pairs to share their *written personal conversion stories* (3 minutes each), emphasizing the spiritual results of that commitment (10-12 minutes).

B. *Study Guide* — "Sharing God's Plan of Salvation," pages 39-43 (present the visual illustration before the entire group, 27-30 minutes).
  • Begin by briefly reviewing last weeks *Study Guide* highlights.
  • Ask your group members to look at the bottom of page 39; then lead them through "A," "B," and "C," emphasizing "B". The key thought to impress on their minds is the importance of *praying* for the opportunity to witness daily. "... *you do not have because you do not ask* " (JAMES 4:28, NIV).
  • Remind them that telling their personal conversion story is often the open door for explaining the full plan of salvation.
  • Ask your group to turn to page 42, then begin your presentation, using the pre-selected visual aid (overhead, chalk board, or flipchart). Move through the Bridge Illustration as if you were conversing with an interested non-Christian. Every time you *refer* to one of the verses, ask someone from the group to *quote* it, then

Session 12

write down the suggested *summary statement* (page 41). After completing the entire presentation, assume that the inquirer has responded favorably and lead him or her through the *sinner's prayer*. Do this by explaining that God looks upon the heart. Then ask him or her to pray after you audibly, one phrase at a time. Conclude by congratulating the inquirer and explaining JOHN 5:24. Be sure he or she personalizes the verse.

• Briefly discuss the class presentation with your group members, showing them Appendix B in the *Study Guide* and reminding them how important it is to keep their eight witnessing verses up to date and usable at all times.

Note: The sinner's prayer should also be memorized. Though the wording can be *varied*, remind them that all seven ingredients need to be included (Confession through Thanksgiving, page 43).

ASSIGNMENT AND CLOSING (5 - 8 minutes)

A. Lead the group to *complete* and *turn in* their pre-addressed evaluation post cards (please mail these cards).

B. Tell the class how to obtain their next *Spiritual Journal* from:
  • the church office, library, or bookstore
  • the publisher (see pre-addressed order card in *Study Guide*)
  • a local Christian bookstore

C. *Assignment*: Continue notetaking, daily *Quiet Times*, and witnessing.
  • Memorize 2 TIMOTHY 1:12b and review all the verses used in the Bridge Illustration. Be prepared to quote several verses next week.
  • Practice presenting the Bridge Illustration twice with friends or family members. You might suggest an approach like this, "I need to learn how to teach a brief illustration explaining the central message of the Bible. Would you be kind enough to help me practice?" When the Lord provides an opportunity, share it with an interested non-Christian friend. Be prepared to present the Bridge Illustration to another class member next week.

- Pray each day this week for natural opportunities to *share a word of truth*. This is the kind of prayer God loves to answer with an exciting "YES"!

Close in prayer, focusing on the wonderful *privilege* of showing others how to go to heaven!

Note to Leader: Next week is your *last* session, so it is time to let your group know about opportunities to continue in Bible study and other elective courses (coordinate this with your church staff). Some suggested options are mentioned in the introduction to this *Leader's Guide* (page 6, and *Study Guide*, Appendix A,). The following chart describes the *Christian Essential's Series* format.

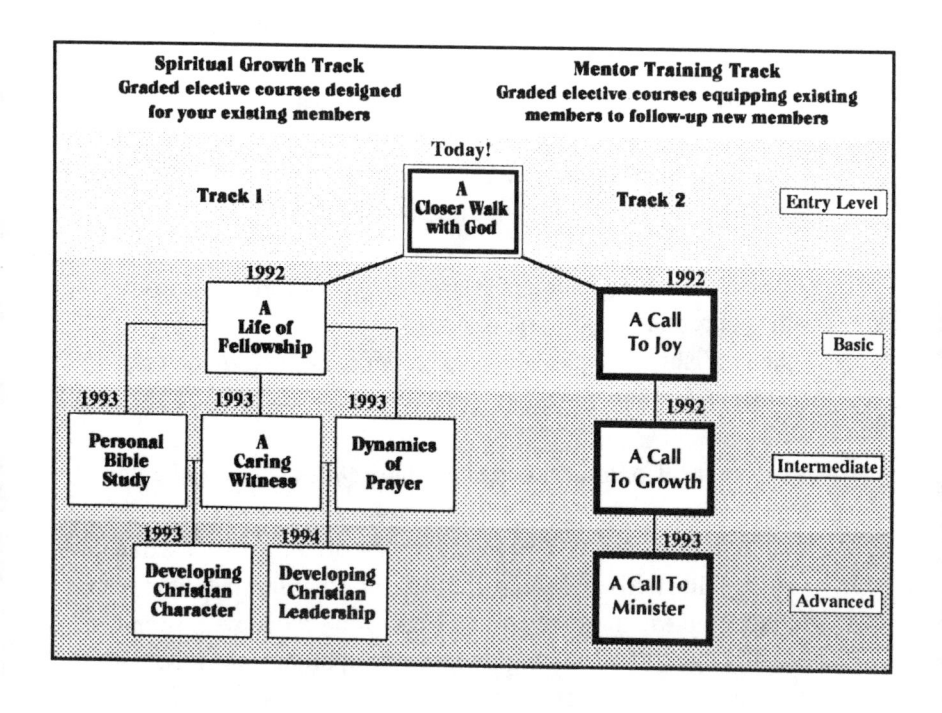

	Spiritual Growth Track Graded elective courses designed for your existing members			Mentor Training Track Graded elective courses equipping existing members to follow-up new members	
			Today! A Closer Walk with God		
	Track 1			Track 2	Entry Level
		1992 A Life of Fellowship		1992 A Call To Joy	Basic
1993 Personal Bible Study	1993 A Caring Witness	1993 Dynamics of Prayer		1992 A Call To Growth	Intermediate
1993 Developing Christian Character	1994 Developing Christian Leadership			1993 A Call To Minister	Advanced

SESSION 13

"For everyone born of God overcomes the world. This is the victory that has overcome the world, even our faith"
(1 JOHN 5:4, NIV).

PURPOSE

A. This session teaches the life-changing principle of living by faith and allowing Jesus Christ to truly be Lord in daily experience.

B. *Challenge* — May each of us leave this course with a strong commitment to live in victory, multiply spiritually, and glorify God in our attitudes and actions!

PREPARATION

A. Read your *Study Guide*, pages 44-49, praying that this last session will be the very best to date. Meditate on the fact that our greatest resource for living a victorious Christian life is the indwelling Christ! No Christian doctrine is more liberating, dynamic, and deeply needed for daily living.

B. Read or listen to the following:
 • Teacher's Preparation Cassette — Session 13
 • *Leader's Guide*, Appendix F — "The Indwelling Christ"

C. If your church plans to offer *A Call to Joy* or other elective courses, they should now be ready to pre-enroll.

D. Read through the class presentation, writing your teaching notes in the margins of the *Study Guide*.

PRESENTATION

A. *Accountability* — Divide into pairs and quote three verses each (including 2 TIMOTHY 1:12); then pray for each other. Ask the Lord to seal the *lessons* of this course in your *heart* for life.

- Exchange reports about witnessing opportunities during the week. Focus on sharing the Bridge Illustration (7-10 minutes).

B. *Study Guide* — "Living by Faith," pages 44-49 (group reading, 25-30 minutes). Supplement the group reading by using your choice of selected illustrations from the *Leader's Guide*, Appendix G.
  - Since this inspiring lesson is so important, go through each section, adding your personal emphasis to the group reading. Save the *personal commitment* (page 49) until the end of the session.
  - You may choose to briefly read portions of Appendix F; if not, seek to practically illustrate this *life-changing* principle from your own experience.
  - Challenge your group to genuinely deal with the relationship between *faith* and *obedience*. Encourage them to consciously plan to live by faith!

FINAL ASSIGNMENT AND CLOSING (10 minutes)

A. Testimonies of intent — Ask how many are planning to keep enjoying their closer walk with God.

B. If practical, pre-register course participants for their next Bible study opportunity.

C. Challenge the class to select a scripture memory plan, and then stay with it (see *Study Guide,* Appendix A).

D. Encourage them to be faithful in seeking to share a "word of truth" everyday as a lifestyle.

E. Close by praying in unison " The Disciple's Prayer" suggested in your *Study Guide*, page 48.

"Being confident of this very thing, that He who has begun a good work in you will complete it until the day of Jesus Christ"
(PHILIPPIANS 1:6, NKJV).

APPENDIX A

THE PUBLIC AND PRIVATE MINISTRY OF JESUS
Billie Hanks Jr.

In public, the Lord carried out an active ministry based upon:
- **Preaching**
- **Teaching**
- **Healing**
- **Miracles**

It would be safe to say that no one has ever preached a message as profound as The Sermon on the Mount, been followed for days by crowds who went without food in order to hear Him teach, healed a man born blind, or walked on water — except Jesus!

His *public* ministry leaves every thinking person in astonishment. Yet, in spite of all He said and did in public, His greatest, but probably His least understood, accomplishment took place almost unnoticed. This was His quiet ministry of training future leaders.

If He had healed all the sick people in His generation, taught the faithful, preached to the multitudes, and performed the world's greatest miracles, yet left *no* trained leaders — the *church* we love today would not exist!

It was His plan to leave behind a team of faithful men and women who would teach others also (2 Timothy 2:2). His first century disciples were ordinary people just like us, but He left them prepared to change the world!

Let's pause for a minute to define terms:

> **Teaching** — The transmission of *concepts*, *ideas*, and *facts*.

> **Training** — The transmission of *learned skills*.

The apostles received the full benefit of both teaching and training. They *listened* to Jesus teach and then learned the skills of ministry by *watching* Him time after time. One form of His instruction depended upon the ear (teaching) and the other depended upon the eye (training).

Note the emphasis in these important verses — The apostles' training came through continued *association* with the Lord.

"Then He appointed twelve, that they might be with Him and that He might send them out to preach" (MARK 3:14 NKJV).

". . . Follow Me, and I will make you fishers of men" (MATTHEW 4:19, NKJV).

Application:
To establish a personal discipling ministry, it is necessary to move beyond today's everchanging trends and methods. Wisdom calls us to build our lives around *time-tested* and proven biblical concepts.

Let's consider four presuppositions:

1. Jesus Christ is, was, and always will be — *God!*

2. Being fully God, yet fully man, He was the *wisest* man who ever lived.

3. Because He was the *wisest* man who ever lived, He knew how to *invest* His life in ministry in the most effective manner. If there had been a better way to accomplish His objective, He would have known about it and used it.

4. By studying His life and ministry, we can apply His apprenticing methodology in our own ministries today. The key is to fully understand that His *life* was as inspired as His *teaching*!

As you lead your class, seek to impart this basic truth — sometimes Jesus ministered:

                One-on-One   **Training**
                One-on-Some   **Teaching**
                One-on-Many   **Preaching**

We need to utilize all *three* of these important New Testament methods!

APPENDIX B

SPIRITUAL FRIENDSHIP WITH NEW CHRISTIANS

Everyone wants close meaningful friendships. Solomon said, *"A friend loves at all times, and a brother is born for adversity"* (PROVERBS 17:17, NKJV). But why is friendship especially important to new Christians? Because most people come to Christ out of a deep sense of need.

Heartache, loneliness, disappointment and even fear often bring individuals to the most wonderful day in their life — their spiritual new birth! *"Therefore, if anyone is in Christ, he is a new creation; old things have passed away; behold, all things have become new"* (2 CORINTHIANS 5:17, NKJV).

At conversion, the new believer is spiritually dependent and greatly needs the support of a caring friend. Isaiah, the Old Testament prophet, pictured this need by writing about Christ as a shepherd and older believers as nursing mother (ewe) sheep.

"Like a shepherd, He will tend His flock. In His arm He will gather the lambs, and carry them in His bosom; He will gently lead the nursing ewes" (ISAIAH 40:11, NASB).

A new Christian needs the protection provided by his shepherd and the nurture of a more mature member of the flock. As church members who have prayed, studied, and personally enjoyed close fellowship with Christ, it is our role to be like the nursing mother sheep.

In nature, it is the mother ewe, rather than a shepherd, who gives special care to a newborn lamb. Loving nurture is provided during the critical months before the new arrival is old enough to feed itself in the pasture. This simple process is natural, personal, and proven by countless centuries of agricultural experience.

Sometimes a lamb will lose or be separated from its mother. This unfortunate situation inspired the lyrics of the famous cowboy song that says, "Get along little dogie. It's your misfortune and none of my own!"

Nowhere in the Bible do we find the suggestion that a shepherd should gather all the new lambs together and attempt to feed them himself. This is only necessary when orphaned lambs have no one else to care.

Over the years a haunting thought has bothered me. Jesus said, "... [if] *you love me,... feed My lambs*" (JOHN 21:15, NKJV). So what does our keep-up-if-you-can, hit-or-miss, fill-in-the-blank approach to nurture really say about our love? How much do we care? What are we personally doing about feeding the new believers?

You may be thinking, "where do I start?" That's the right question, because God loves His lambs, and follow-up is a simple ministry that all of us can enjoy. *Friendship* is the place to begin!

First, make yourself available. You can tell your pastor or the appropriate staff member of your church that you want to help a new believer or a new member feel secure in his or her faith and the new church family. One good *friend* can make all the difference!

Second, pray expectantly and prepare for the exciting privilege of investing time in another person's life. Take advantage of every opportunity to be *trained* in the use of good follow-up materials. While it is friendship that counts most, the materials will provide a natural way to focus on Christ.

Third, plan to show your new friend how to have a daily *Quiet Time*, take sermon notes, and witness. In doing this, simply be yourself and always try to be practical in dealing with temptation and the "how-to's" of prayer, Bible study, and everyday Christian living.

Fourth, and perhaps most important, remember that the Holy Spirit will enable you to teach, love, correct and counsel beyond your own ability; so simply move ahead in faith, remembering Paul's reassuring words, "*I can do all things through Christ who strengthens me*" (PHILIPPIANS 4:13, NKJV).

If each of us begins this simple practice, the Lord's lambs will grow and multiply, and before long, there will be millions of healthy Christians

Appendix B

sharing the good news; but if we fail to extend a helping hand, the results can be tragic! Even now, North America's largest evangelical denomination cannot find approximately 40% of its members.

Some missing members have been victimized by cults, others are spiritually sick due to malnutrition and still others have gone back into a life of sin and defeat. They have the power to live in victory, but no one has drawn close and taught them how to *appreciate* and *enjoy* what is already theirs in Christ!

Backsliding, as it is sometimes called, is not so much the failure of new believers as it is the failure of the church. Backsliding often occurs when members are too preoccupied to look after their greatest responsibility — caring for the Lord's lambs.

Charles Finney, the great 19th Century evangelist once said,

"When the hearts of converts are warm with their first love, then is the time to make them fully acquainted with their Saviour, to hold Christ up in all of His grandeur, so as to break the power of sin forever — to lead them to break away from all self-dependence and to receive Him as a present, perfect and everlasting Saviour."

"Unless this course is taken, their backsliding is inevitable. You might as well expect to roll back the waters of Niagara as to stay the tide of their former habits. Surrounded as they are with temptation, they need a deep, thorough and experiential acquaintance with the Saviour. If they are left to their own resources to stand against temptation instead of being directed to the Saviour, they are certain to become discouraged and to fall into bondage."

Experience has shown that Finney's wise words were true both then and now!

We need to personally pray for a heart like Sam Jones, the 18th Century country preacher who said, "I never see a poor, weak brother that I don't wish I had nothing else in the world to do but keep him away from temptation and keep him on the straight and narrow until he gets his feet firmly planted on the ground. They need nursing, they need your help. Oh, what's the use of bringing them into the church if nobody takes care of them? My dear brethren, you who are spiritual, love the new convert. Stand by him, and do your best for him."

In my experience, doing one's best is not too hard when love is the motivating factor. Follow-up is natural, and the friendship that is developed during a new believer's most teachable months is rich and rewarding!

This may come as a surprise, but you are probably much better prepared for a ministry of follow-up than you realize. Why? Because your life is your most important asset. The Bible teaches us to use our *example* as an investment in the lives of others. Paul drove this truth home when he wrote:

"Whatever you have learned or received or heard from me, or seen in me—put it into practice. And the God of peace will be with you"
(PHILIPPIANS 4:9, NIV).

What really happens in a discipling relationship? PROVERBS 27:17 describes it in graphic terms, *"As iron sharpens iron, so one man sharpens another"* (NIV). We learn from one another as we seek to grow in faithful obedience to Christ.

Today, some of my closest friendships are the result of the happy experience of simply seeking to witness, follow-up, and disciple newer believers.

As those you help learn to help others, God's spiritual family grows, and your joy grows with it!

Jesus said, *"If anyone loves Me, he will obey My teaching..."* (JOHN 14:23, NIV). In that spirit of willful obedience, are you ready to begin proving your love by feeding His sheep?

APPENDIX C

THE BURDEN OF MY HEART
Billie Hanks Jr.

The Vision For Multiplication

"And this gospel of the kingdom will be preached in the whole world as a testimony to all nations, and then the end will come" (MATTHEW 24:14, NIV).

On a sunny Florida afternoon years ago, I heard the haunting and unforgettable words of a leading evangelical British minister who said, "Mark my words, North American Christians: Your large church buildings will be as empty as the cathedrals of Great Britain within a span of 25 to 50 years if you do not change your methodology."

The well-known cleric spoke with the assurance of a prophet, yet the humility of one who had been mellowed by many years of Christian service.

Our Traditional Methodology

We must resist the temptation to rely on the baptism of our church children to exonerate us from our larger call to national and world evangelization, and we must also carefully re-examine our own methods of evangelism to see whether they are based on tradition or on the Bible. Our almost exclusive dependence upon evangelism by *addition* through preaching is reminiscent of the days when throngs of people listened to the eloquent messages of such greats as England's Charles Haddon Spurgeon. One cannot help but ask the question "Why?" What is the basis for our philosophy of ministry? Why are we content to simply *add* new members?

The academic instruction of our Christian leaders at the college and seminary level continues to focus on theological concepts and scholarship while all but overlooking practical instruction in how to *equip laypeople* for their ministries. As a result, few laypeople know how to evangelize, nurture, or disciple others for Christ. At a time when the world birthrate is growing faster than at any other point in history, the absence of personal follow-up and apprenticeship in equipping the laity at a local church level all but ensures a serious, long-range decline in church membership.

One day I was invited to lunch by one of England's leading young evangelists. Over the meal we discussed evangelism in our two countries and denominations, comparing various approaches and methods from his Anglican perspective and my Baptist background.

After graciously complementing my denomination as one of the world's most evangelistic, he asked me a most penetrating question: "What percentage of your Baptist laity would normally win someone to Jesus Christ during any given year?"

At that point I wished he had asked about our generous giving to missions, our popular evangelistic conferences, or our city-wide crusades, but he had asked a question that was most embarrassing.

I had to tell him that even in our best years fewer than 5 percent of the laity and clergy combined led anyone to a saving knowledge of Christ. We simply do not have enough *trained* workers. In Christendom, we have an army of unequipped people who are sympathetic with evangelism but only a few who are participating in the joy of the harvest! Many bystanders are praying for these workers. They appreciate what the workers are doing and even help pay their wages, but they do not know how to *participate* in the harvest.

As I have travelled and ministered as the guest of numerous Christian groups, I have discovered that this is an unsolved church problem worldwide. Too few are doing the work of many in evangelism! Consciously or unconsciously, we have wasted our most valuable resource: *the laity.*

Relying upon our traditional approach, which neglects personal follow-up and fails to utilize our more mature laypeople, we are plagued with a growing attrition rate, no matter how successful our short-range evangelistic efforts may appear. Because of this unattended problem, large percentages of our congregations have become inactive and many members cannot even be found. Obviously, the new converts who never grow will never win another to Christ. It needs to be understood that evangelism's most persistent *enemy* is poorly planned and poorly executed follow-up.

The Evangelized as Evangelizers

The real issue involved in making disciples is international in scope and is critical in terms of the future of the church. The task of educating, motivating, and equipping the laity for a lifestyle of ministry is far larger than any single denomination, organization, or program. Something of this magnitude requires the joint effort of all Christians and a return to the biblical principles used by the early church.

Since theological education is the pacesetter in evangelism and methodology, it bears a major responsibility and obligation to be balanced, practical, and scripturally sound in its approach to disciplemaking. The need is urgent because the methods which we have inherited from tradition are simply not working in terms of the Great Commission. We must learn from the failures of the past and open our minds to the fact that parts of the world that were once Christian, now desperately need to be re-evangelized. The best efforts of our Reformation forefathers were not enough to sustain evangelism from generation to generation.

We must take strategic steps in our churches, colleges, and seminaries to ensure that Christians of this generation receive instruction in how to have a quality ministry of *spiritual multiplication*. Dr. Herschel H. Hobbs has wisely said, "The work of evangelism is never complete until the evangelized becomes the evangelizer." Amplifying this statement, if the process of making disciples is to be complete, all new Christians should be trained to be active in evangelism themselves. This full circle apprenticeship process requires time, love, discipline, and personal instruction. The added work of discipleship is well worth the investment because the fruit remains and multiplies.

The church's great evangelistic task will be carried out only when we update our philosophy of ministry through a re-examination of the *principles* revealed in the ministry of Christ. The gospels show us that Jesus trained His disciples by *association* before giving them the Great Commission. Being with Him was their primary means of learning how to minister. Mark tells us, *"He appointed twelve...that they might be with Him and that He might send them out to preach"* (MARK 3:14, NKJV).

The disciples' evangelism grew out of a lifestyle seasoned by many hours in Jesus' presence. They were apprenticed in real life situations.

They *saw* evangelism, counseling, preaching, teaching, and every other form of ministry first-hand.

Jesus' pattern was *"Come, follow Me, . . . and I will make you fishers of men"* (MATTHEW 4:19, NIV). He showed them how to minister. By contrast, as church leaders we typically *tell* people why they ought to minister, but fail to *show* them how.

Great preaching and teaching are absolutely vital, but they cannot replace the apprenticing concept demonstrated by Christ. The critical need of the modern church does not involve moving away from preaching and teaching, but it does require re-establishing a New Testament concept of apprenticeship.

Under staff leadership committed to this revitalized approach, church members will be trained and shown how to carry out their God-given ministries (see EPHESIANS 2:10). Until this happens, widespread evangelistic multiplication will not occur in the church, and the average believer will never know the joy of leading another person to Christ.

Taking God's Mandate Seriously

Billy Graham has said, "One of the first verses of scripture that Dawson Trotman, founder of the Navigators, made me memorize was *'The things that thou has heard of me among many witnesses, the same commit thou to faithful men, who shall be able to teach others also'* (2 TIMOTHY 2:2,

Appendix C 55

KJV). This is a little like a mathematical formula for spreading the gospel and enlarging the church. Paul taught Timothy; Timothy shared what he knew with faithful men; these faithful men would then teach others also. And so the process goes on and on. If every believer followed this pattern, the church could reach the entire world with the gospel in one generation! Mass crusades, in which I believe and to which I have committed my life, will never finish the Great Commission; but a one-by-one ministry will" (*The Holy Spirit*, Word Books, 1978, p. 147).

I am in deep agreement with Dr. Graham that evangelism by *addition alone* will not reach the world. The burden of my heart is to see the concept of *multiplying disciples* restored to our churches again, because it alone has the realistic potential of actually reaching the entire world with the gospel!

Our present short-range course of action more often than not breeds a sense of frustration and spiritual fatigue in the lives of faithful Christian workers. Because of the lack of a long-range strategy, many Christian workers find themselves totally absorbed in a multitude of good activities to the exclusion of the *best*! We find no time for training our future lay leaders for the work of ministry. This omission leaves a pastor and his staff without a strong base of qualified laypeople to labor with them in the ministries of the local church. As a result, paid staff members often end up carrying out the church's follow-up, counseling, hospital visitation, and evangelistic ministries largely on their own.

Since many Christian workers find no time for personal involvement in equipping new Christians, the vicious cycle repeats itself again and again!

We dare not become too busy to follow Jesus' example. The Lord revealed His personal pattern of ministry by *investing* His maximum time in the lives of those who would bear the maximum responsibility in the future ministry of the church. The result was men like Peter, James, and John; and the process began as soon as they responded to His call.

Our lack of immediate follow-up through friendship leaves some of our best lay leaders unfulfilled, because their spiritual gifts remain undeveloped and unused. When our people fail to receive a workable strategy for personal ministry, they settle into a life of churchmanship rather than disciplemaking. Because of this failure, many new Christians are neglected and are left wide open to an assortment of groups with false doctrines that thrive on the biblical ignorance of immature but wellmeaning church members. The tragedy is that a high percentage of new believers never receive the sound instruction or loving care of a more mature Christian.

If we will learn to be with people, equipping them as Jesus did, and long to see new Christians perfected in Christ as Paul and Barnabas did (ACTS 14:21-23), our generation can *expect* to see the greatest multiplication of converts and congregations since the early days of the Christian faith.

Love, vision, personal discipline, and the willingness to accept mutual accountability are the critical factors required for a lifestyle that produces spiritual multipliers. It is sobering to think that until Christian leaders take seriously God's mandate to equip His people, Christ's second coming may actually be postponed. His return is dependent on world evangelization (MATTHEW 24:14), and world evangelization is dependent on His saints (EPHESIANS 4:11-12) being equipped and carrying out their ministries.

Distinguishing Teaching from Training

Many of the church's evangelistic failures of the past have resulted from attempting to impart through *teaching* those skills which were designed to be transmitted through *training*.

Teaching requires the transmission of ideas and concepts. A gifted teacher can hold the attention of tens, hundreds, or even thousands. Typically, words are used to convey his thoughts, and he needs little else to get his point across. Our Lord was a master teacher; His illustrations and parables are beyond equal. The size of the group He spoke to had no bearing on His ability to clearly express the truth. He was comfortable with twelve or a gathering of well over five thousand. His teaching of the Sermon on the Mount points out that any size group can be taught

Appendix C 57

spiritual truths as long as they can hear and want to hear what is being said (MATTHEW 5:1-2).

This is not true with training, however. *Training* requires the transmission of learned skills. The term that best communicates this concept in many cultures is apprenticeship. Because observation and practical experience are needed for effective training to occur, one-on-one relationships are universally used as the accepted apprenticing format.

In Jesus' ministry of instruction, He was sometimes with His disciples in a group, and at other times with them individually. He discipled them on both levels, and ultimately they became very effective witnesses.

Consider the practice of medicine. Surgeons who perform the most delicate surgery are required to have the longest and most personalized periods of intern training. In general, the more critical the consequence of failure, the greater the need for individual instruction.

If for no other reason than this, training in evangelism, which involves *eternity*, must demand our very best and most committed effort! The Lord's clear emphasis on training emerged early in His ministry.

> *"As Jesus was walking beside the Sea of Galilee, He saw two brothers, Simon called Peter and his brother Andrew. They were casting a net into the lake, for they were fishermen. 'Come, follow Me,' Jesus said, 'and I will make you fishers of men.' At once they left their nets and followed Him"* (MATTHEW 4:18-20, NIV).

Their on-the-job training had begun, and this school lasted until Christ's ascension!

Some Observations on the Disciple Making Process

If any single factor has hampered churches in establishing good ministries of follow-up, it is their lack of concern over trained disciplers required for individual care. If your church is facing this problem, let me offer a liberating and encouraging solution.

It has been my observation that spiritually mature lay leaders are the product of a large number of *unstructured* teaching and training relationships that have come about through the various ministries of the church. Therefore, even though they may not have *formally* received one-to-one training themselves, they are nevertheless potentially prepared to follow-up new and growing believers if given the benefit of simple instruction and guidance in that direction.

In reality, many laypeople already possess a high percentage of the knowledge required to follow-up a new convert. The lacking ingredients are simply vision, organization, and access to the proper tools.

As a group leader you can enjoy two levels of ministry. You can *teach* the philosophy of discipleship and explain its spiritual disciplines. But beyond that, you can personally *follow-up* and *apprentice* one or two laypeople each year on a one-to-one basis. You will be encouraged to know that hundreds of lay leaders are already experiencing the spiritual rewards and evangelistic results afforded by this simple approach to ministry.

A second liberating concept can be described in this way: The more *mature* the Timothy, the less structured the relationship. It has been my privilege to be trained by seven men in my Christian life. Several of them are still living and are my closest friends. The relationship that started out in a structured manner has steadily grown into a deep friendship as the years have passed by.

In a church setting, basic follow-up will typically last only a few weeks, but a true *apprenticing relationship* will involve months or even years.

Our Spiritual Objective:

We should expect some observable results but should always teach and train with the awareness that we are growing an oak tree. Spiritual maturity is a process that is steady, fulfilling, and effective. If impatience characterizes a ministry, that ministry will tend to focus on *events*, rather than a long-range disciplemaking process. Visualize a *rope* with several knots in it. Which is more important: the knots or the rope that connects them? If the knots symbolize events and the rope symbolizes the equipping process, then both are essential!

It is good to have a variety of events in the life of a church, but these events–though meaningful at the time–lose their *long-range* effectiveness unless they are connected to one another by an effective multiplication and equipping process.

I once talked with a pastor who had been meeting one-on-one with several of his key members for five years. The expected fruit from his ministry was all there—except for *evangelism*. He wondered why.

Through our discussion I learned that he was merely *teaching* his people about evangelism rather than *training* them to witness. All their activities were related to Bible study, scripture memory, prayer, and character development. We must not assume that witnessing skills will spontaneously develop as a result of these other disciplines. Although these activities are very important and they develop depth and faith, ultimately we must take trainees out of the church building and practice witnessing if we want them to become evangelizers.

Two of the best known ministries that work on this apprenticeship principle of on-the-job training are Evangelism Explosion and Continuing Witness Training. We have discovered that they are both ideally suited for personal follow-up. Their emphasis provides instruction in threshold visits and direct evangelism, while a course like *A Call To Joy* provides instruction in how to follow-up and then apprentice a new convert for a *lifestyle* of spiritual growth and evangelistic multiplication. It is as if the Holy Spirit merged these two emphases in order to underscore the need for a full cycle of evangelism in the church.

A Ministry for Anyone:

Another exciting observation is the fact that even a very small church can begin the disciplemaking process. My first pastorate was a church with only seven members, but in that rural community God gave me the opportunity to disciple a young turkey farmer who had a tremendous desire to grow in Christ. If you don't have enough people to teach a course on spiritual multiplication, you can still successfully start the process with only one person!

People of all ages can enjoy follow-up and become disciplemakers. A friend told me an exciting story about a seventy-eight-year-old woman in a wheelchair who was meeting individually with five women in her home, one each weekday. Only the aspects of the process, which involved making visits, were left to others.

When asked why she had never taught a Sunday school class, she replied, "I am timid before a group, but I like helping one person at a time." She added that she wished someone had shown her the importance of personal ministry years before, so she wouldn't have wasted so much valuable time.

Age makes no difference, and being in a wheelchair need not hold anyone back. Some of the best follow-up and discipling being done today is carried out by *retirees* who have much spiritual wisdom to share with a younger generation of believers.

A last observation has to do with the time period in which a discipler should be assigned to work with a new member. The minister of discipleship in a large church in New Mexico once shared some revealing statistics with me. Their research with four hundred new Christians above the age of fifteen underscores the importance of immediate follow-up. It was discovered that of the new Christians who met with their discipler during the first week after joining the church, **90 percent** completed their basic follow-up instruction. Of those who did not get started until the second week, **70 percent** completed the training. Of those who did not begin until the third week, only **30 percent** completed their training, and serious attrition was evident!

Every pastor, staff-member, and lay leader can have a vital part in changing the local and global statistics which indicate that we are currently losing the battle during an hour of unprecedented opportunity. It is we who are shaping the very foundation of the future church, just

Appendix C

as the Reformers once molded and shaped the church that we love today. The awesome reality is that God has committed the spiritual destiny of millions into *our* hands — we are His ambassadors.

The gauntlet of spiritual leadership has been passed to our generation, and we must make an important *decision* regarding methodology. Every year that passes makes the right decision even more critical. A rising percentage of the world's population does *not* yet know Jesus Christ. Consider your own country and city for a moment—is this not true? We are standing at an eternal crossroad!

However good the method of *addition* has been, it has not been good enough. By itself, it has proven inadequate. Today's situation calls for a new daring, new vision, and a return to a full-orbed New Testament philosophy of ministry. We must harness the power of *evangelistic multiplication* and commit ourselves to the long-range strategy of equipping all the Lord's people to be spiritual reproducers.

We have the Word of God, the Holy Spirit, two thousand years of church history, and the privilege of prayer as our resources—we *can* each effect personal change and the whole world will feel it as we multiply.

At this moment the choice is yours!

Note: We encourage you to read selected portions of this message to your class as you feel led. We pray this will help build a foundation for *The Christian Essentials Series* course entitled *A Call To Joy*. May God bless you with many lambs that grow and multiply!

". . . go and make disciples of all nations . . ."
MATTHEW 28:19 (NIV)

APPENDIX D

SHARING CHRIST NATURALLY

The three sessions on evangelism can be a real turning point for many class participants. The key is to move from theory to practice. Seek to help each class member feel at ease by being transparent. If they have ever battled with timidity or fear, let them know that they are in good company!

Next, lead them to see that witnessing really isn't nearly as hard as they think. Focus on God's part of the process by reminding them that He:
- *produces the opportunities*
- *prepares each heart*
- *provides the words and wisdom.*

They are merely to share the truth and leave the results to God, allowing the Holy Spirit to do His work.

There is little that can *excite* the heart of a Christian like praying with someone when that person gives his or her life to Christ! As your class members pray and prepare for this wonderful privilege, God will begin to honor their faith.

Let the joy and overflow of each experience encourage the group. Their seeming failures may be important stepping stones to success, so don't let them be discouraged. Use every opportunity to build a spirit of participation.

> **"As iron sharpens iron, So a man sharpens the countenance of his friend"** (PROVERBS 27:17, NKJV).

Beyond these suggestions, we hope you will recruit your graduates for outreach visitation or the evangelism training opportunities in your church. Many will be spiritually motivated as they leave this course and will be ready to take their next step with Christ; so we pray that you will *challenge* them to follow His leading and share their faith as a *lifestyle*!

APPENDIX E

MY PERSONAL CONVERSION STORY

1. My life before becoming a Christian.

2. How I realized my need for Christ.

3. Why I accepted Christ as my Lord and Savior.

4. When and how that decision was made.

5. Specific ways Christ has changed my life since I became a Christian.

6. What the Lord is teaching me now.

APPENDIX F

THE INDWELLING CHRIST

When you teach these verses:

- **GALATIANS 2:20**
- **1 THESSALONIANS 5:24**
- **PHILIPPIANS 2:13**

you will be presenting the secret to living a victorious Christian life. The issue is not learning to *try* harder, but to *trust* more! This blessing occurs when we discover and appropriate the vital truth that Christ actually lives *in* us.

Christ indwells us (through the work of the Holy Spirit) from the very moment we turn away from sin and self, making Him our personal Lord and Savior.

Think back – do you remember your time of decision? Do you remember the change that began (**2 CORINTHIANS 5:17**)? It started by faith and it continues by faith today!

Growth is a daily decision. When we let Christ *reign* in our attitudes and actions, we grow; but when we seek to live, give, and work *for* Him, the results are very disappointing.

We soon discover that spiritual success comes only when we look to Christ and trust Him to *do* the doing in and through our lives. He *is* our Christian life (**JOHN 15:5**)! He is the *source* of all He calls us to be and the *strength* for all that He calls us to do.

Everything that we ask for in God's *will* is possible (**1 JOHN 5:14**). The point is never to take life into our own hands. We are to seek to do His will, in His way, in His time. Willful obedience equals true freedom, and spiritual dependence equals a powerful, successful Christian life. This paradox makes living by faith difficult for people to understand until they actually experience the wonderful results of doing it!

To illustrate this liberating concept, let me share the true story of a friend from Great Britain. Charles Price writes, ". . . on one of my frequent absences from home, the grass on our lawn was in need of cutting. We had recently purchased a new motor mower, which my wife Hilary had seen me use several times. Knowing I would not be back for several days, and fine weather was not likely to last until then, she decided to mow the grass. The mower was fairly solid, with rotary blades, roller and petrol motor weighing down on the machine. She started the engine, which automatically began to turn the blades in its stationary position, and then began to push. It was really hard work! To get any movement took almost all her strength, but determined as she was, she applied all her might and with all her body against the mower at a forty-five degree angle she gave it everything she had until after two lengths of the lawn she was exhausted!

"This was very confusing. She had seen me walking up and down the lawn behind the mower, apparently effortlessly. Although she knew I was stronger than she was, she also knew the difference wasn't as great as this! In frustration and anger she grabbed hold of the handle to give the machine a good shake and in so doing caught the clutch lever and engaged it. Suddenly the mower took off across the lawn under its own power, cutting the grass in its path with Hilary flying out behind it almost horizontal to the ground! What a marvellous difference!

"How frustrating to find yourself manually operating something designed to run on its own power! And how wonderfully liberating to discover after a long, hard, tiring struggle that there are resources at your disposal you knew nothing about. This has been the personal experience of many people right through history. They have tried with the utmost sincerity and dedication to do for God what only God himself could do for them. There was no fault in their zeal or failure in their enthusiasm. They just did not know or *appropriate* the indwelling presence of God himself, as the only One who can provide what it takes to accomplish his will. When out of despair and exhaustion they find Christ to be alive in them, the discovery has been revolutionary.

Appendix F

"There can never be any significant *progress* in the Christian life until a fundamental discovery has been made and appropriated: '*It is no longer I who live but Christ who lives in me*'" (Galatians 2:20).

> Thank you for teaching *A Closer Walk with God*. May your life be enriched every time you lead a group on this spiritual journey!

APPENDIX G

LESSON ILLUSTRATIONS

SESSION 1

Selected Illustration from *If You Love Me*
- The value of taking notes, pages 7&8
  (A cowboy whose cup had a hole; *Study Guide*, page 5, F)

SESSION 2

Selected Illustrations from *If You Love Me*
- The example of Jesus (Mark 1:35), pages 14&15
  (He started the day with the Father; *Study Guide*, page 6, 1)
- God desires our fellowship, page 22
  (Love is spelled T-I-M-E; *Study Guide*, page 6, b)
- Our need for direction, pages 23&24
  (King David's experience; *Study Guide*, page 6, c)
- Practical devotions, page 16
  (Discover your biological clock; *Study Guide*, page 7, 2)
- Dry spells (Psalm 127:2), page 25
  (Everyone's problem; *Study Guide*, page 8, 5, a)
- Getting started having a *Quiet Time*, pages 17&18
  (You must make the decision to begin; *Study Guide*, Page 9, b)

SESSION 3

Selected illustration from *If You Love Me*
- Put others first (Matthew 7:12) – page 36, #5
  (The responsibility of knowledge; *Study Guide*, page 10, A)

SESSION 4

Selected illustrations from *If You Love Me*
- Guard your affections (Colossians 3:2), page 30, principle #3
  (Christ must come first to be Lord; *Study Guide*, page 14, A)
- Your thoughts (Proverbs 23:7a), page 31

Appendix G 69

(Your mind is the mirror of your affections; *Study Guide*, page 15, B)
- The secret of pondering (Psalm 46:10a), pages 87-91 (Mary's meditation is our example; *Study Guide*, page 15, D)
- The secret of godliness (1 Timothy 4:7b), page 21 (The positive impact of obedience; *Study Guide*, page 16, VI)

SESSION 6

Selected illustrations from *If You Love Me*
- Communicating Love for God, pages 40&41 (the highest form of prayer; *Study Guide*, page 19, 1)
- Growing in adoration, pages 44&45 (Even lost people will offer adoration; *Study Guide*, page 19, 1)
- Confession and Repentance, pages 61&62 (God wants to forgive us; *Study Guide*, page 19, 2)
- Why Confession works, pages 62&63 (Christ our Savior; *Study Guide*, pages 19, 2)
- Praying against idols, page 76 (A wife and daughter who prayed; *Study Guide*, page 19,3)
- When you don't know how to pray, pages 51&52 (the fable of two monks; *Study Guide*, page 20, 4)
- How to pray in hard times, page 53 (Mature petitions; *Study Guide*, page 20, 4)
- The results of ingratitude, page 69 (The heavenly host illustration; *Study Guide*, page 20, 5)
- Barriers to gratitude, page 68 (Works, pride, and immorality; *Study Guide*, page 20, 5)

SESSION 8

Selected illustration from *Leader's Guide*, Appendix B
- Shepherd, Ewe and Lamb; *Leader's Guide,* page 47 (*Study Guide*, page 27, C)

SESSION 9

Selected illustrations from *Leader's Guide*, Appendix C
- British minister quote, page 51
  (*Study Guide*, page 29, V)
- Distinguishing teaching from training, page 56
  (Discuss differences, Surgeon training; *Study Guide*, page 30, 3)
  (Effect on witnessing skills, page 59; *Study Guide*, page 30, 3)
- Seventy-eight-year-old woman, page 60
  (God can use people of all ages; *Study Guide*, page 31, 5)

SESSION 10

Selected illustrations from *Everyday Evangelism* and *Leader's Guide*, Appendix D
- Well trained cutting-horse, *Everyday Evangelism*, page 43
  (*Study Guide*, page 37, B)
- Victory over fear, *Everyday Evangelism*, page 50, #3
  (Depend on Me!, 2 Timothy 1:7; *Study Guide*, page 37, B)
- God's part of the process, *Leader's Guide*, Appendix D, page 62
  (*Study Guide*, page 37,1)

SESSION 11

Selected illustration from *Everyday Evangelism*
- Sharing Christ Naturally, page 60
  (Flow, river, flow!, dammed up Christian life; *Study Guide*, page 39, B)

SESSION 13

Selected illustration from *Leader's Guide*, Appendix F
- Appropriating the indwelling presence of God, pages 66&67
  (Charles Price illustration; *Study Guide*, page 46, B)

ADDITIONAL NOTES and PRAYER REQUESTS

ADDITIONAL NOTES and PRAYER REQUESTS

ADDITIONAL NOTES and PRAYER REQUESTS

ADDITIONAL NOTES and PRAYER REQUESTS